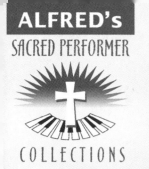

ALFRED's
SACRED PERFORMER
COLLECTIONS

What *Praise* Can I Play on Sunday?
Book 4: July and August Services

10 Easily Prepared Piano Arrangements

Arranged by Carol Tornquist

I have been a church pianist from a very young age, playing various styles of music from classical pieces, to hymns, to gospel songs. By the time I became involved in Christian music publishing as an arranger, praise music was emerging as the most popular musical expression of worship. Its singable melodies and catchy rhythms produced a musical style accessible to musicians and congregations alike. Today, praise songs are being sung and listened to not only on Sunday mornings but practically anytime and anywhere.

In creating this series, I have chosen the best praise songs, and they are recognizable to most congregations. Each arrangement is easy to prepare and tastefully arranged in a contemporary style appropriate for Sunday morning worship services. Book 4, for July and August, features solos for the Fourth of July as well as general (non-seasonal) selections. Other books in this series are as follows:

Book 1: January and February
Book 2: March and April
Book 3: May and June

Book 5: September and October
Book 6: November and December

I hope pianists will find this series to be a perfect all-in-one resource for the entire church year.

Carol Tornquist

Produced by
Alfred Music Publishing Co., Inc.
P.O. Box 10003
Van Nuys, CA 91410-0003
alfred.com

Printed in USA.

ISBN-10: 0-7390-8408-9
ISBN-13: 978-0-7390-8408-3
Cover Photo: © iStockphoto.com/mycola

Amazing Grace (My Chains Are Gone)

Words and Music by Chris Tomlin and Louie Giglio
Arranged by Carol Tornquist

With emotion (♩ = ca. 76)

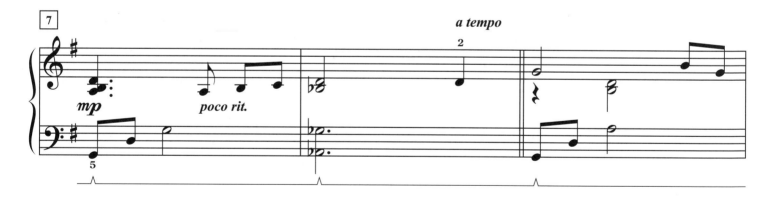

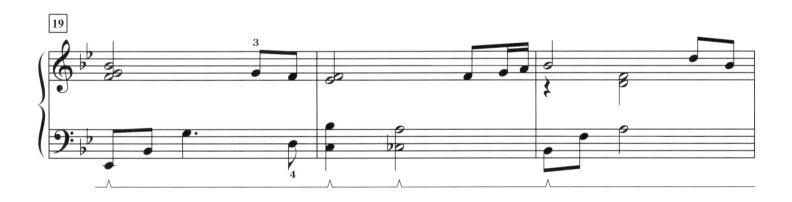

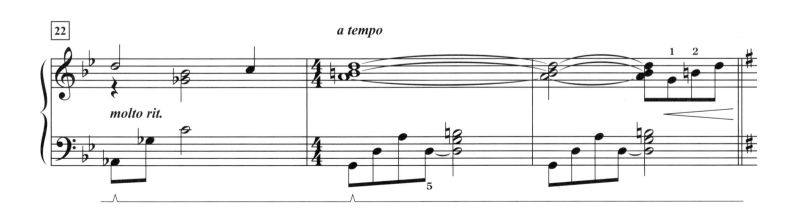

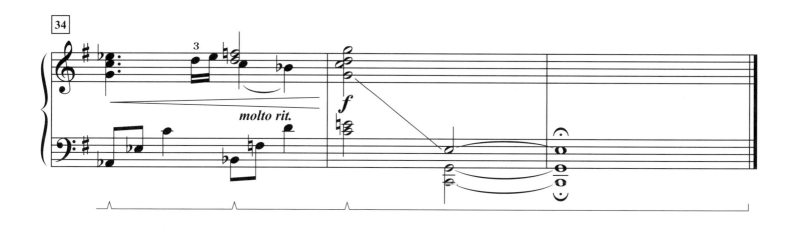

Enough

Words and Music by Chris Tomlin and Louie Giglio
Arranged by Carol Tornquist

Flowing (♩ = ca. 84)

(Approx. Performance Time – 2:00)
General

Ancient Words

By Lynn DeShazo
Arranged by Carol Tornquist

With reverence (♩ = ca. 72)

(Approx. Performance Time – 2:15)
General

Blessed Be Your Name

Words and Music by
Beth Redman and Matt Redman
Arranged by Carol Tornquist

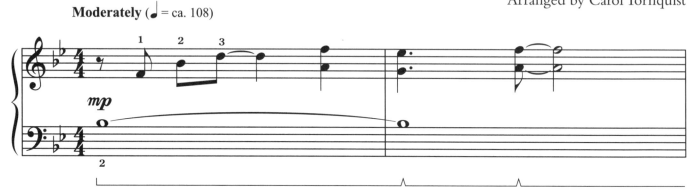

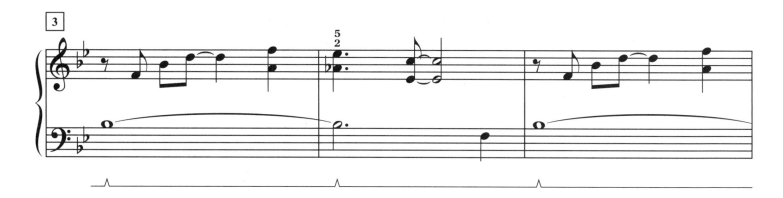

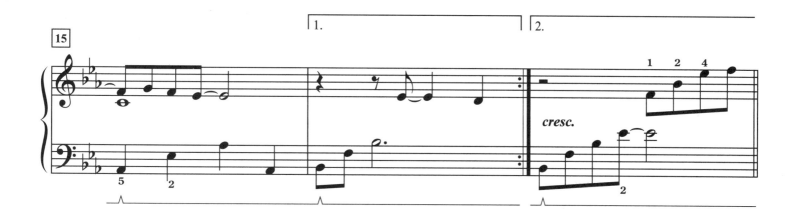

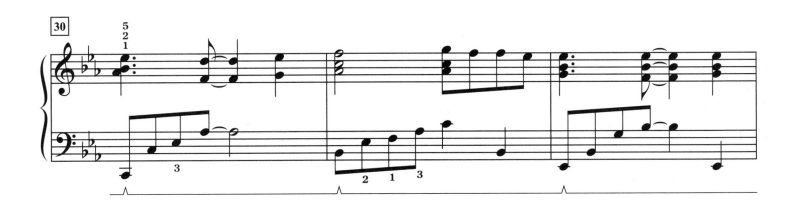

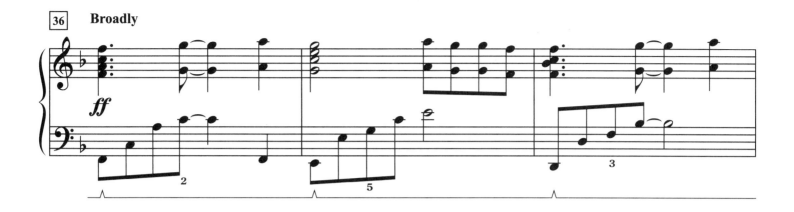

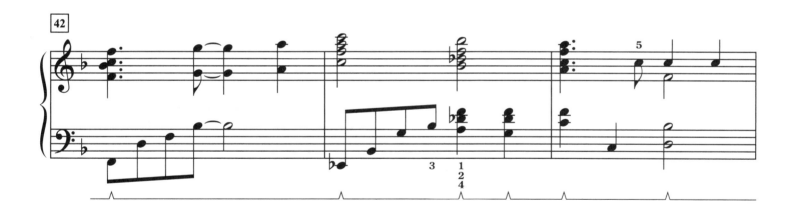

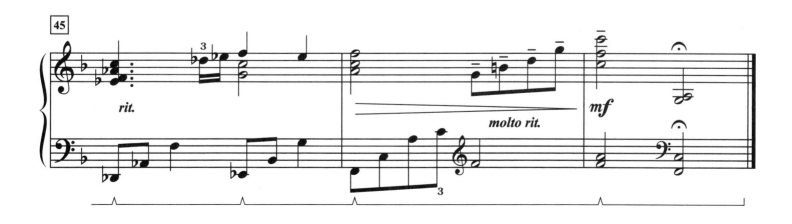

(Approx. Performance Time – 2:15)
Communion

Come to the Table

By Claire Cloninger and Martin J. Nystrom
Arranged by Carol Tornquist

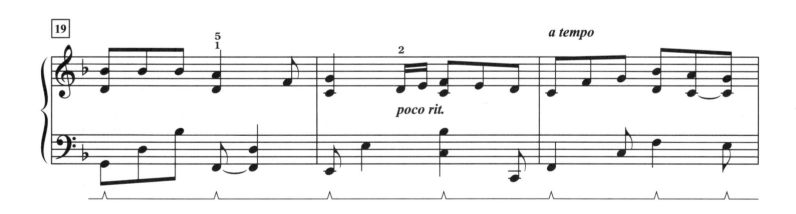

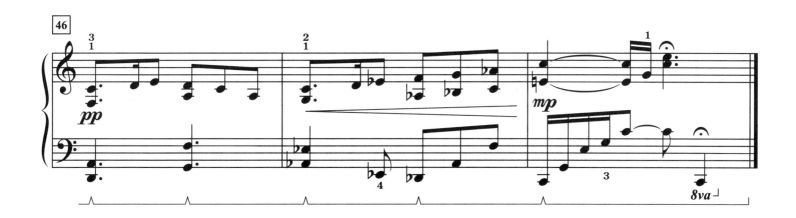

I Can Only Imagine

Words and Music by Bart Millard
Arranged by Carol Tornquist

24

(Approx. Performance Time – 2:45)
The Fourth of July

Shout to the North
with
My Country, 'Tis of Thee

Moderately, in two (♩. = 54)

"Shout to the North"
Words and Music by Martin Smith

Arranged by Carol Tornquist

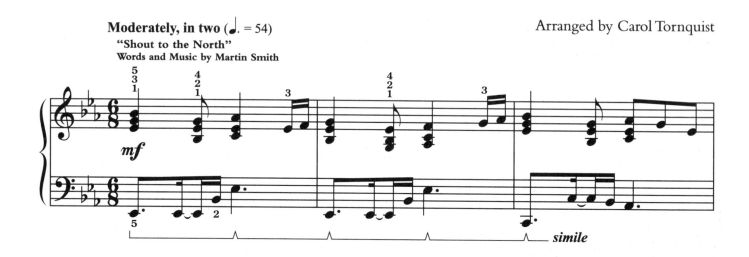

"My Country, 'Tis of Thee"
Music by Samuel F. Smith
Music from *Thesaurus Musicus*

(Approx. Performance Time – 2:00)
The Fourth of July

29

Let Freedom Ring

Words and Music by Dennis L. Jernigan
Arranged by Carol Tornquist

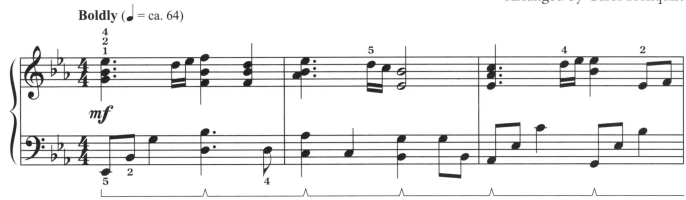

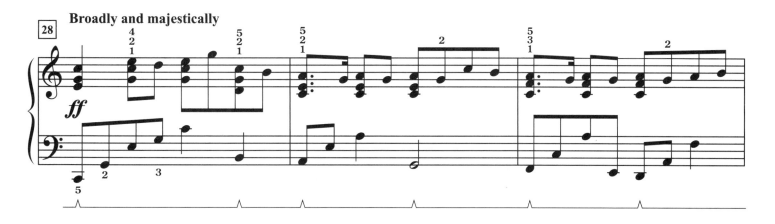

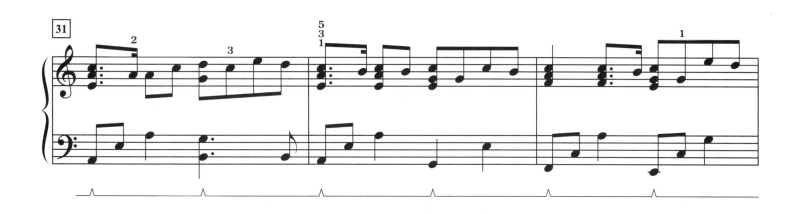

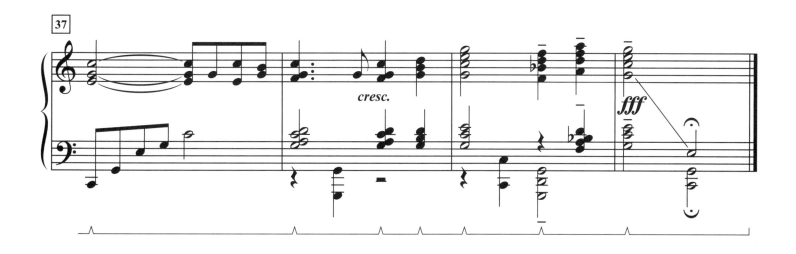

(Approx. Performance Time – 2:30)
General

Let It Rise

Words and Music by Holland Davis
Arranged by Carol Tornquist

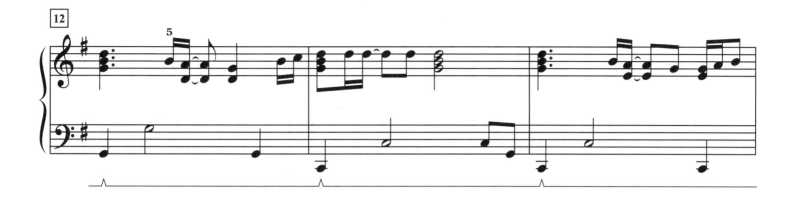

34

(Approx. Performance Time – 3:00)
General

You Are My King (Amazing Love)

Words and Music by Billy James Foote
Arranged by Carol Tornquist

Slowly and deliberately ($\quarternote$ = ca. 64)

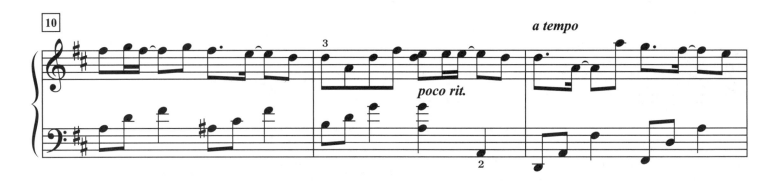

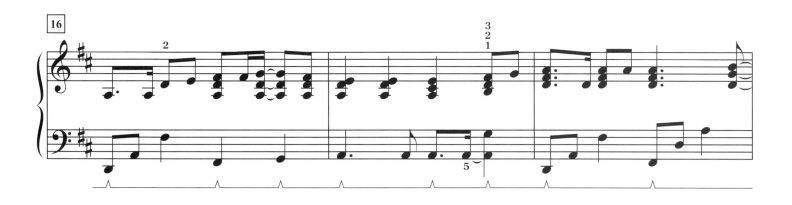

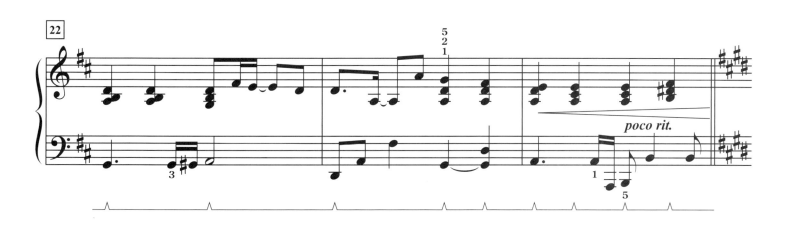

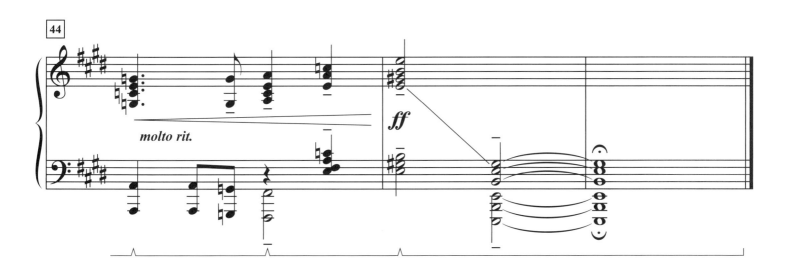